I'm
Celebrating

By Ann Kiemel

I'm Celebrating

Ann Kiemel

Fleming H. Revell Company
Old Tappan, New Jersey

Quotations from *hi! i'm ann* by Ann Kiemel. Kansas City, Mo.: Beacon Hill Press of Kansas City, 1974. Used by permission.

Quotations from *I'm Out to Change My World* are used by permission of Impact Books, a Division of John T. Benson Publishing Co., Nashville, TN 37202. Used by permission.

Photographs by Fred Kiemel

Library of Congress Cataloging in Publication Data

Kiemel, Ann.
   I'm celebrating.

   1. Christian poetry, American.   I.   Title.
PS3561.I34514   811'.5'4   79-10400
ISBN 0-8007-6010-7

TO mollie, from my neighborhood.
she found Jesus this year.

& to my world, boston.

i'm celebrating.

send up a hundred balloons. paint a sunrise in the sky. throw flowers to the wind. grab somebody's hand and squeeze it. wrap an arm around a heart. wear sunshine in your eyes. touch a small child's face.

sing to the world, "JESUS IS LOVE. HE CHANGES EVERY-THING."

i'm celebrating.

stand tall. keep your head high. believe for a bigger mountain. shake your fist at the attempts of satan. dare to dream. reach on your tiptoes. color the walls with love.

call out to the neighborhood, "I BELIEVE. I CARE. I WALK WITH YOU. JESUS DOES."

i'm celebrating.

children can sing. old men can be brave. broken hearts can heal. disillusioned minds can be cleared. lonely voices will be heard. impossibilities will vanish. young and old and rich and poor and healthy and weak can stand together. side by side. as one. without fear. with patches of blue and brand-new tomor-rows.

i'm promising, "IT'S OKAY. DON'T BE SCARED. JESUS WILL NOT FAIL."

i'm celebrating.

Jesus has come. to an old, beautiful city—my world. to beating hearts: vibrant and strong, unsteady and fearful. down dark, forbidden streets and quiet, empty corners. over tea and warm cookies. on the subway and in the corridors. in old, beat-up cabs.

remember, "NEVER GIVE UP."

i'm celebrating.

because i am just one, everyday young woman. just ann. and though the world is so wide, it does not matter. God is bigger, and He dwells in me, in you. dreams will live. you'll see.

i'm shouting, "FOLLOWING JESUS PAYS."

i'm celebrating.

the climbing of hills. the simplicity of children. the quiet of sometimes being alone. the dawn after the dark. getting up after falling down. lessons following failures. wearing a ponytail. putting on tennis shoes and running. knowing when my best is terrible, God's grace still stands. baking cookies. feeling peace after obeying. having the courage to say *no* when it's hard.

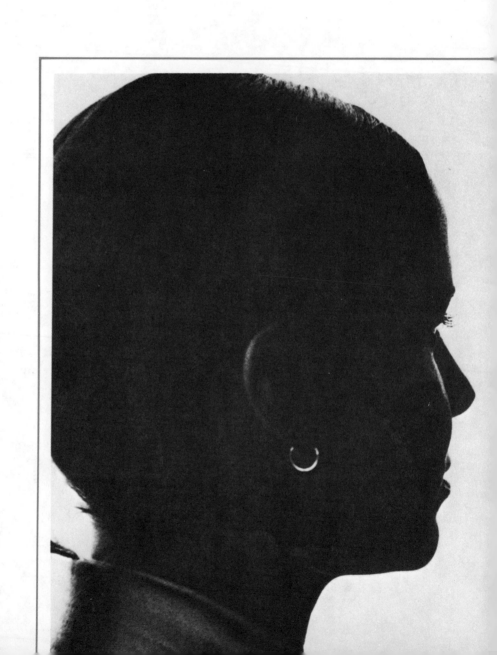

Please...you celebrate, too!

you can. it was God's idea you should. the world is silent and morose and depleted and waiting to hear your laughter and your shouts and your echoes of praise and thanksgiving.

eyes are glazed. hearts are tired, beating slowly. thousands dress up and cover up and work over all their empty places and unheard cries.

the world is *waiting* to hear your song. to see the wonder in your eyes. to touch the music and feel it, too.

i am going to change my world.
you watch.
you'll see.
because i have a giant of a Lord
inside of me,
and He and i with love
will push through the barriers.
i'm not afraid.

i am Jesus to the world around me.
you are.
His heart and hands and eyes and voice
and spirit of honesty and care.
you and God and i . . . a team.
    we can love the world to joy, and meaningful and
        brand-new tomorrows.
    Jesus dreamed we would.

i stand before Christ and the world. my heart shouts
an affirmation:
   "Jesus, i am a humble, lowly servant woman.
      take me . . . all of me.
   add anything. take away anything.
      at any cost. with any price.
   make me Yours. completely . . . wholly.
   may i not be remembered for
      how i wear my hair
      or the shape of my face
      or the people i know
      or the crowds i've addressed.
   may i be known for loving You . . .
      for carrying a dream . . .
      for building bridges
   to the hurt and broken and lost in the world.
   make me what You would be if You lived
      in Person where i do.
   may everything accomplished through my simple
      life bring honor and glory to You.
   take my human failures and flaws,
      and use them to remind these who know me
      that only You are God,
      and i will always just be ann.
        amen.
        amen."

I'm going where He goes—
out into the world
of lonely people.
"Sir, can I take your hand?
Or yours, ma'am?
Can I walk with you?
Can I laugh with you
and cry with you
and love you to Jesus?"

You just can't stop love.
It crushes barriers.
It breaks and builds bridges.
It finds a way through.
It never gives up.
It's hard work.
It listens.
It walks ten extra miles.
It's something you do.
Jesus did it for me.
He died to set me free.
He lives to share my life with me
and I go to His
and my
people
and love wins.

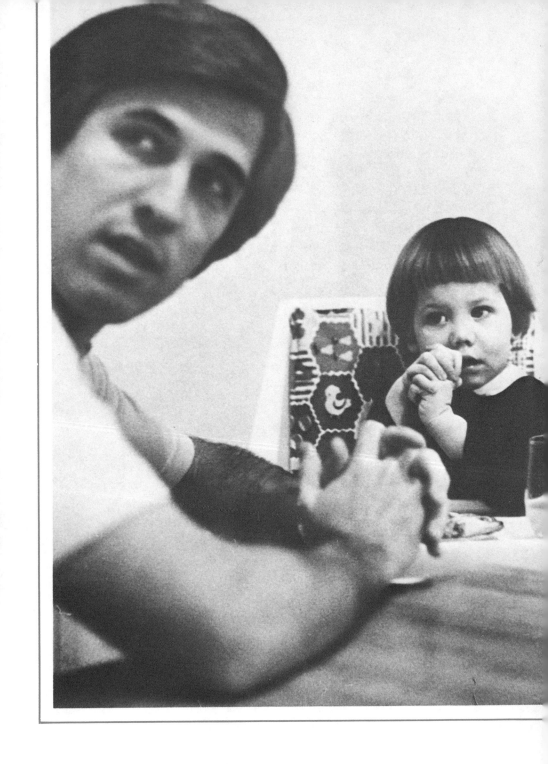

God and i, with love,
will change our world because
i believe in the kind of Christ that
chose common men—fishermen—
probably men with dirt
under their fingernails . . .
and some teeth missing.
because they loved Him it was YES, LORD,
to everything He asked of them.
He used 12 common, ordinary men
to literally move the world.

---

the motto of my life is YES, LORD.
anytime, anywhere.
"yes" to whatever He wants, wherever He leads.
sometimes i have kind of died inside, saying "yes." it has
                                                    meant,
"God, you can put anything in or take anything out of my
life . . . anything You wish . . . if you will help me."

YES to hurt.
   i have been hurt. everyone has.
   sometimes by people who know they are doing it,
but many times by events or circumstances of which
   others are unaware.
one of my greatest shocks has been learning that i've
   hurt people the most through some gesture or word
   of which i was not even conscious.
that is why i cling to honesty. however painful,
   i beg people to tell me how they really feel.
   to be open. to show me where i've hurt them.
how can i help something i don't know about?

If you have eyes to see
or a little boy next to you
or if you have someone to call a friend
if you felt the warm sunlight in your face today
or saw the blue sky and laughed
you must know what it means to sing
"God is so good."
If you know what it feels like to laugh with God,
to have fallen flat on your face
and have Him reach out
and say I still love you, take my hand;
to feel Him lift your guilt,
to ease your pain,
to have Him soothe your tired,
worn, broken heart,
then you must understand how good He is.

oh, i wish for hours and hours of gentle spirits and
easy laughter. clear eyes and warm handshakes.
   forgiving hearts and unselfish pocketbooks.

---

hours and hours of little touches of brilliance
   in everyday history.
      mary and her perfume.
         paul and a song in jail.
            Jesus spending the afternoon with
               zacchaeus
   or washing the tired feet of His followers
   or simply holding a child
         on His lap.

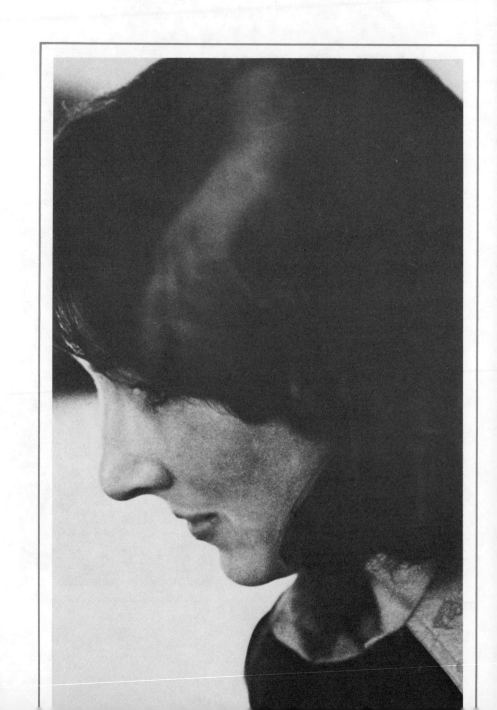

i love that word impossible because my God believes in
    adventure
        and extraordinary mountains, and He dares
to be alive in a world crawling with terrible
                                                situations.

---

simple, strong hope . . . "God gives a song"
for a little boy in chicago, cold.
an old man in a convalescent home who feels rejected.
for you who feel insecure or unlovely or unwanted or
    maladjusted or misplaced,
and me.
a song right where we need it,
a new song . . . people unafraid to reach out and wrap their
                                                arms
around someone or take a hand or smooth a brow.
a song that makes us one.
    that gives us power to believe in a better world.
    that follows someone to their secret, silent hiding place
        where they weep and almost gag out their grief.
to them . . . may the brave new song come through.

Love is hard work.
You know something else?
Love never gives up.
I wonder how many people are willing to say,
"Oh God,
I want more love today and tomorrow than I ever had before.
Oh God,
I want greater faith.
I want to believe you're a bigger God
than I ever believed you were before.
God, I'm just one person,
but God you can count on me.
If you'll fill me,
and walk with me,
you can count on me, God."

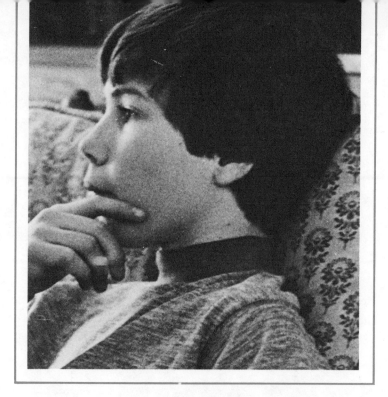

when i was a small girl, my father would say,
    "ann, it pays to serve Jesus. . . ."
i would respond,
    "why, daddy . . . ? i am nine years old, and
    ugly, and hardly anyone likes me."

and he'd smile, and tousle my hair, and say,
    "GIVE GOD TIME. . . ."

give God time.
i wish it were simple . . . i wish that patience
    had been born in my
        heart and mind and veins.

the LONG HAUL is what really matters.
today, i am thirty, and i can say,
    "daddy, you were right . . . Jesus has
        changed the color of EVERYTHING."

all the people in the world
who have poured their BEST into every day,
and given years of earnest service in Christ's Name,
must be very cherished by Him.
He always judges our hearts
more than the visible results.
the church janitors and streetsweepers and
    bricklayers
and gas station attendants and factory workers . . . well,
who ever decided that THEY
aren't the great people of the world?
    that THEIR ideas don't have the
        greatest weight?

maybe . . . someday . . .
    i'll sell all i have and go live in the ghetto.
    or speak on foreign soil . . . across the globe.
    or lead a "change the world" crusade in america.
    or talk about Jesus on the johnny carson show.

but today . . . it's being happy being ann.
    accepting my skin and my hair and my looks.
    feeling freedom walking down the street in
    my neighborhood and yelling "hello" to
    all the people i know . . .
    and singing little songs in God-ordained
    moments . . .
and being. just being.
    with wide heart and straight back
    and a quality of spirit that says to
everyone i meet:
    God is love and He makes people whole.
    Jesus changes *everything.*

love heals prejudice
  because love accepts people where they are.
    how they look, how they act, what their potential is, or
                             isn't.
    it makes no demands, no stipulations. it constantly
      reaches out and says, "you may be at one pole and i
      at another . . . but can we be friends
      and learn from each other?"

You can do one of two things in your world.
You can build a wall
or you can build a bridge
to every person you meet.
I'm out to build bridges,
are you?
Come and build bridges with me.

loving one another—
that's where evangelism begins.
how
can we change our world . . .
if we cannot even care about each other in our
    own circle?
pick a growing church in the New
    Testament.
how about thessalonica? everyone poured in,
not because the sunday school teacher was
    so fantastic,
or the curricula . . . or even the program.
they didn't even bring in a special musical
    group.
but . . . wow, how they loved one another!

I see people—
    warm faces,
        a running tear,
            a small child's hug,
                an old man's gnarled grip of love.
Saroyan said,
    "People is all there is—
        and all there was—
            and all there ever will be."

            People—
      that's all that matters to me
        that Jesus be Lord
         and people.

i believe in a BIG GOD.
i don't decide to witness tomorrow morning.
instead i make hope and laughter and peace
    and poise and caring concern
a way of life with me . . .
because God is . . .

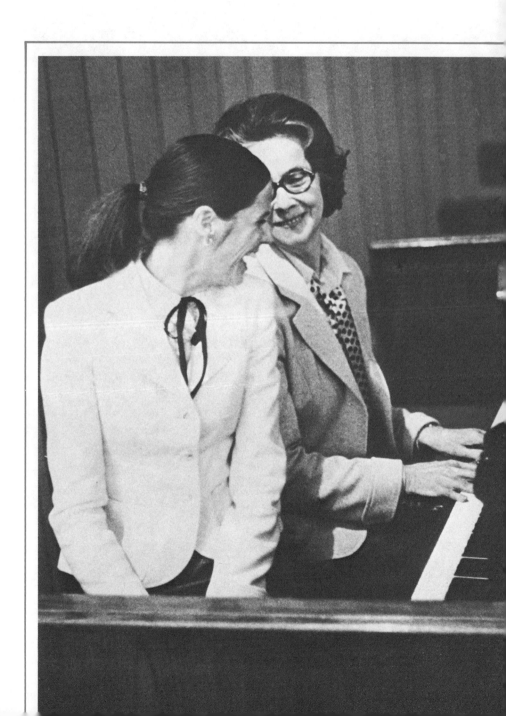

justice stands
    immovable, for right,
and has no tolerance for wrong.
however long i live, i will believe
    though, that God, who is love, will always have mercy
    with His justice. He finds fault in us, but He does not
        tear down.
He seeks to bring love
                and to mend
                        and heal.

        love cares about people.
        what they feel.
        where they live.
        how they hurt.

love is also open to criticism, and considers that there is usually *some* truth in it.

love accepts the fact that mistakes and failures and blunders are real, and love appreciates constructive, not distorted, openness.

i need you to dream with me.
i need you to believe in a great Lord
with me.
i need you to love me in my world.
i need you to walk down the street
and reach out and say,
"hey, brother, may i take your hand
and walk with you?
and you, sister, and you?
may i laugh with you
and cry with you,
and may God and i share
your lonely roads with you?"
you and God
with love
can change **your** world, too.

47

i do think there are miracles of new cars and nice
   houses
      and surprise visits from extraordinary people.
   BUT the greatest miracles, for me,
   are the paralyzed people who can still laugh and
      shed warmth,
         and create . . . those who lose loved ones
and don't remain bitter and questioning the rest of
   their lives,
      but rather allow God to work it for good. . . .

to love means to be vulnerable . . .
    to allow God to put in
        or take out of our lives
            whatever He knows will make us sensitive to
                His Spirit,
                    and to a dying world.

often people talk of being afraid of God.
i'm not. people, yes. God, no.
God knows me through and through. He's fair. He's kind.
and forgiving and longsuffering. He places no stigmas, ever.

the next time i start to put down
                              or withdraw
              or be indifferent toward someone,
i hope Christ, the compassionate Receiver, reminds me
        with painful awareness,
                              how much i have hurt
when i have felt rejection.

God really loves me. He really does.
He laughs with me . . . cries with me.
He pushes the hair out of my eyes.
He understands. He does!
and who can resist LOVE? who?

oh, i always want to wear a smile
reach out for a strong handshake
and look people square in the eye.
to laugh easily.
   listen carefully.
     meet people's needs
     right where they are . . .
       in Christ's Name.

Jesus, make my heart wide.
so wide that differences don't matter.
just beating hearts and minds.

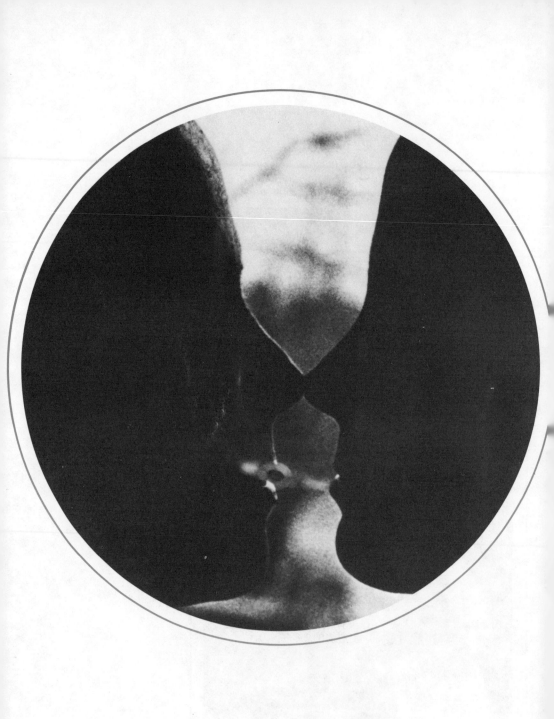

it doesn't matter how much love we give to
one other human being . . .
   unless that person is willing to start loving
     back . . . to begin planting seeds of love
      in his or her own back yard . . .
     there can be no healing.

"Jesus, i like what i am because it was Your idea. help
me to find adventure in my uniqueness, and not
want to be what someone else is. God, if i lose sight of
the fun of being me, then Your dreams of what i can be in
the world will die. always help me to remember, that
this is Your way of being creative."

as a child, my parents talked often about the secret to life:
letting Jesus be Lord. today i have little assurance about
MY ability to cope successfully with all that shall face me in
life. i am more convinced than ever that if Jesus Christ controls
me totally, and i faithfully seek Him, He will move quietly and
constantly and protectively through
   the valleys
      agonies
         decisions
            incredibly stifling places.

if you WANT to,
you can be happy wherever you are.
but then,
it all depends on how hard
you are willing to work at it.

at times, people are physically healed.
i've been. it could never be a difficult task for God.
but it's not His highest gift.
Christ's tenderest extending of Himself to us
is His ability to take us as individuals,
        to know us through and through,
            and to choose, out of extraordinary love,
His highest gift, separately,
                            uniquely.
sometimes life. sometimes death. sometimes an added portion
of love.
but always what is best for us and those who love us.

i know what it is to love someone.
to laugh easily.
to bury my head and cry hard if i like, unashamed.
to talk plainly and bravely about gut-feelings.
to be unafraid of desertion.
but when those i love hurt, so do i.
their causes become my causes, in some form.
their disappointments and injustices are absorbed right in
                                                          with
my own. i cannot be removed . . . disconnected.

i really believe the happy people . . .
  people we all like being around . . .
    those who conquer good over evil,
those are the people
who have learned to laugh
easily . . . to find humor . . .
  who never allow satan the advantage
    of dragging their spirits to the ground.
  of thinking he's the winner.

---

i love the word impossible. i'm not an extraordinary person.
i'm a young woman with a simple heart. i live in a huge world
where i walk down the street unnoticed. i board airplanes, lost
in the crowds of passengers. but with God there are no
impossibilities. give up? never. what is my dream? my aim?
victory. because God and i—with love—with sturdy hearts,
and determined daring faiths—will move the world.
        you watch.
                you wait.
                        you'll see.
                                we can.

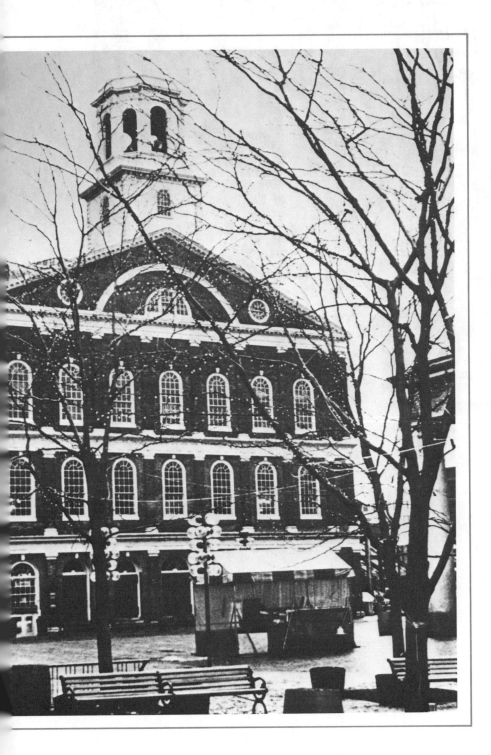

A lot of times you tell people God is love.
      And they laugh.
"Are you kidding me?
      Do you see where I live?
          Did you see my Dad beat me last night?
      God is love?
          I don't buy it."
The only love people in your world will understand is you.
      God and you loving them.
          Then they'll believe.

---

to learn to love must involve being vulnerable to
life. to learn to forgive is being real. to feel compassion
is first to know pain and hurt. it is getting down where
most of the world lives and absorbing their wounds. it
is the Holy Spirit alive and at work in our lives.

times of pain are so hard.
   they take so much courage.
   like today.
but pain is important.
   dreams are made from conquering pain . . .
   from the ability to draw a PLUS across it.
   to cancel out the black, and fill it instead
   with color . . .
whatever that experience is.

the awesome power of the Holy Spirit tearing at our
   lives . . . breaking us into a thousand pieces . . .
      and as my friend bill jackson says . . .

   "i lay before Him, completely naked . . .
      a sinner who needed grace.
      a warrior who needed new life:
         Holy Spirit energy that fleshes itself out
   to kids and gas station attendants and ice cream men
      and waitresses . . .
   a love that fears no evil,
      that laughs at the meager attempts of satan,
         that stands before a mountain and says,
      'in the Name and power of Jesus, move,'
      and the mountain crumbles,
      is leveled to the ground."

And so many mornings, I'd say,
     "Mom, I don't want to go to school today."
And she'd push me out the door
     with my brother and sister and say,
"Don't you kids know
     that life is made up of ordinary days
          when there's no one to pat you on the back?
     When there's no one to praise you?
          When there's no one to honor you?
     When there's no one to see how brave and noble you
                                        are?

Almost all of life is made up of ordinary days.
     And it's how you live your ordinary days
          that determines whether or not you have big
                                        moments.
     Get out there
          and make something of your ordinary days."

how i carry
my cross
will depend upon
the quality of my relationship
with Christ.
an extraordinary one
is my desire.
why compromise for mediocrity
when all of heaven and earth
were brought together
to make God personal to us?

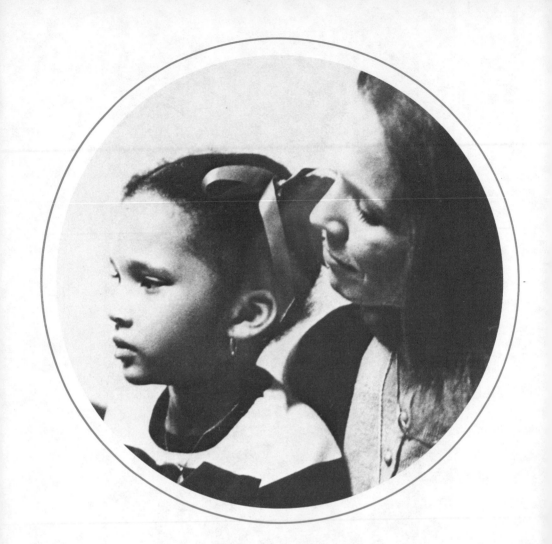

YES.
i'm committed to the Cross . . .
to a price that must be paid,
   a cause worth dying for.

i'm committed to sacrifice . . . to the long haul . . .
   to laying down my life even as Jesus did . . .
   to realizing there are a lot of losses for every
   important gain.

i believe people can care about people. we can be at totally
opposite extremes, and still be friends . . . still belong
together and laugh together. you may not like me as a speaker,
but you can see me as a person. no stereotypes or cubbyholes
                                                          to
stuff me in, or i you.
    just people with hurts and dreams and despairs.
    belonging in His Name.

---

most who are lauded for greatness have rooted it in
        individuality.
sometimes the rareness of personhood that makes a person
        stand out in a crowd
changes once the crowd rallies around. it suddenly seems
necessary and important to "click" with everyone, and then,
suddenly, the rarity gets lost and colorless in total uniformity.

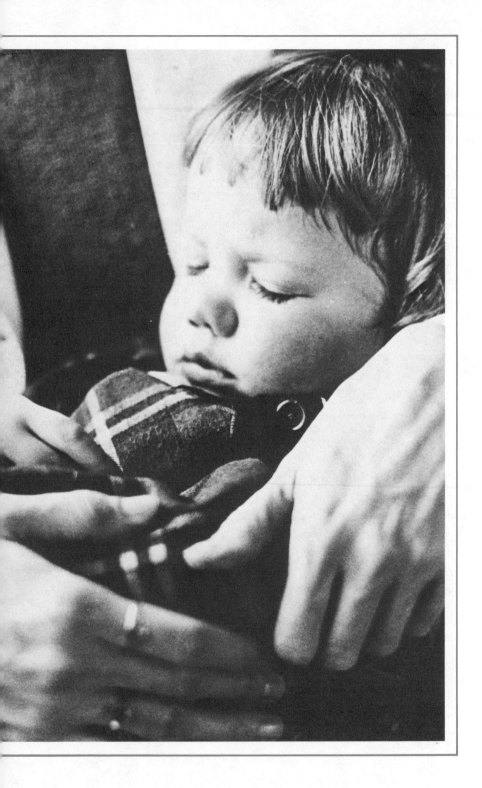

as a young woman, i must internalize for myself what i shall
live and die by.
i must open myself wide to God and decide
through all the varying feelings and opinions and
interpretations what is honestly right and real for me, what
will be true to my integrity.

there are many i call my friends. we laugh a lot. we sip tea, munch good food, and discuss our successes or politics or clothes or others.

but there are very few of my friends i will turn to if i fall flat on my face or get lost in the fog. there are hardly any i totally trust. people who will never commercialize on me. people who know how brash the world can be. people who will believe in my basic good when the bad is showing.

my father is a pray-er.
when my brother was three, someone asked him what
his father did, and he thought a minute and said,
"he prays . . ."
smile.
over and over, mother told us growing up,
   "we'll all make it to heaven
      because of daddy . . . daddy's prayers will
         bring us all through. . . ."

i want time to reveal that
i've done my best . . .
   that Jesus has found me trustworthy . . .
that every day is sobering and exciting.
my race isn't finished yet.

---

when children hear their parents pray,
it makes a difference. there is something about
an honest prayer from fathers and mothers that
makes a child want to be
something better.

thank You, Jesus, very much
for hope in our world
today.
thank You, Jesus,
that we don't have to be
defeated by obstacles.
thank You, Jesus, that we,
with Your love,
can push through every barrier
and crush every obstacle
and can really change our world.

Oh, Jesus, Alleluia.
Thank you
for laughing with us
and crying with us
and walking us to the kingdom of love.
Fill us with your Spirit.
When we're scared give us courage
when we're weak make us strong
when we want to hate give us love and patience.
And may we wrap our arms around somebody
and love them to you.
May we cry with them as you cry with us,
and laugh with them as you laugh with us.
And may they know you by your love in us.
And that you and I and our brothers in love
can change the world.

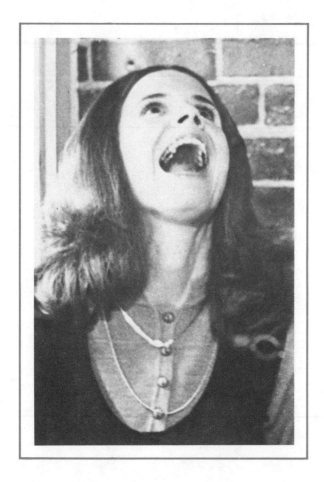

I Choose to Be Happy.

some people think I was born happy: bred a pollyanna. that joy and enthusiasm and momentum are just naturally a part of my veins and my soul and my heart.

that is not real. that does not happen to anybody. when i was small, my mother reminded me over and over that most of life goes on in my mind, and not my heart. that i *choose* to be happy or unhappy. positive or negative. growing or stilted. critical or affirming. creative or indifferent. silent or with a voice to be heard.

many times i have failed. you would probably desert me if you knew how many. but all my life, i have *tried* to choose faith over doubting. easy enthusiasm and warmth over petty moods. hope in the face of despair. believing in opportunities in the midst of impossibilities. i have tried because i believe that is God's will,

> and i know God has all the resources and power to do
> the surprising and beautiful "beyond anything we could
> ask or hope for or believe: infinitely beyond . . . ."

sometimes, it's been tough. in moments, i wanted to give up. i
felt so inadequate and insignificant and very alone. i've been
tired. at times, i've really believed my boat would sink and the
waters would wash over me, and i've screamed, "Jesus, where
are You? i cannot feel You or hear You or understand You."

but those are just small places in life. the hills. the crooked
corners now and then. some exhausting races that must be run
to check commitment and trust and stamina. afterwards, for
miles and miles, the sunrise has come, *always*.
   singing is heard
   in the hills.

today,
i celebrate *you*.
my friends.
fellow dreamers.
determined, faithful followers of Jesus Christ.
people who believe. who are not ashamed to say so.
who will not quit. who remain pure and uncontaminated
even when others beg you to compromise. who follow
your dreams and fight for them and die with them
   so deeply enrooted in you that they spring
      up in other voices and other hearts for
         centuries to come.

i celebrate because we stand together.
without being united, dreams cannot live.
and
as long as i breathe and move,
and even in the darkness when i cannot move,
i will celebrate
most of all
the power, grace, patience and forgiveness
of my loving Savior, Jesus Christ.
He is the Author of all my dreams. of every song.

"surely goodness and mercy have followed me
   all the days of my life . . ."

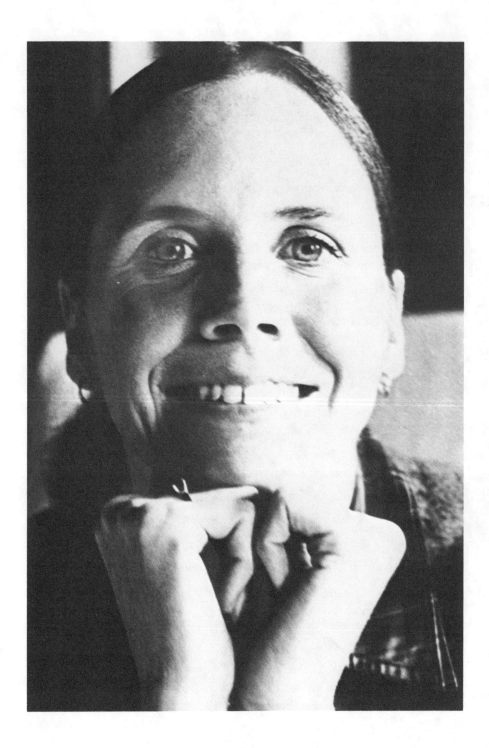

Illustrations

faces—i must open myself to God
    8 ann,   10 ann,   12 ann

prayer—it makes a difference
    15 tre and tom,   17 tre,   18 tre and tom

friends—gentle spirits and easy laughter
    23 sally,   24 raymond,   24 hattie,   27 ruth,   28 sally

neighbors—love accepts people where they are
    31 ann and joanne,   32 mark,   34 vicki

family—you just can't stop love
    36 ann and dad,   37 dad,   38 tre,   39 ann and tre,   40 ann and mother,   43 ann and mother,   44 fred and tre

children—Jesus . . . simply holding a child
    47 ann at children's haven, boston,   48 tre and ashley,   49 children of the neighborhood

on the waterfront—out into the world
    50 waterfront travel service,   52 ann on an old barge

action—God and i . . . will move the world
    54 ann playing tennis,   55 neighborhood hockey player,   56 ann jogging,   57 ann playing tennis

sisters—can I laugh with you . . . ?
    ann and jan,   61 ann and jan

visions of the city—i am going to change my world
    62 tony,   63 boston cab,   64 quincy market,   65 hancock tower and turreted church,   67 fanevil hall,   68 boston street scene,   71 park st. church,   72 aerial view,   73 church window,   75 tower

caring—take a hand or smooth a brow
    76 ann and neighbor,   77 ruth and infant,   78 ruth and ann,   80 tre sleeping,   83 ann and neighbor,   85 ann and virginia in the mirror

saying good-bye—Oh, Jesus . . . . Thank you . . . .
    87 ann playing tennis,   88 ann and suzanne,   90 ann and maintenance boy,   91 ann laughing,   95 ann